national**care**standards

early education and childcare up to the age of 16

dignity —

privacy —

choice —

safety —

realising potential —

equality and diversity —

© Crown copyright 2005

ISBN: 0-7559-4539-5

Scottish Executive
St Andrew's House
Edinburgh
EH1 3DG

Produced for the Scottish Executive by Astron B40112 03/05

Published by the Scottish Executive, March, 2005

Further copies are available from
Blackwell's Bookshop
53 South Bridge
Edinburgh
EH1 1YS

Contents

Introduction

national**care**standards
early education and childcare up to the age of 16

Introduction

Childcare up to age 16 early education and childminders

The national care standards for childcare cover services for children and young people up to the age of 16 years which are to be regulated under the Regulation of Care (Scotland) Act 2001 ('the Act'). They apply equally to services operating in the public, private and voluntary sectors, and in domestic or non-domestic premises which provide services for over two hours a day and for six days or more each year. The range of services covered include:

- nursery classes;

- crèches;

- childminders;

- after school clubs; and

- playgroups.

The national care standards

Scottish Ministers set up the National Care Standards Committee (NCSC) to develop national standards. The NCSC carried out this work with the help of a number of working groups. These groups included people who use services, their families and carers, along with staff, professional associations, regulators from health and social care, local authorities, health boards and independent providers. Many others were also involved in the consultation process.

The starting point for the working group for early education and childcare was a review commissioned by the Scottish Executive. This outlined standards and guidelines used by local authorities to regulate childcare. The working group also took account of quality assurance schemes operated by the Scottish Childminding Association, the Scottish Pre-School Play Association, the Scottish Independent Nurseries Association and the Scottish Out of School Care Network. The standards are also underpinned by *The Child at the Centre*, which is already well established as a tool for self-evaluation in the pre-school centres.

The standards have been developed from the point of view of the user of the services – whether that is the child or young person, the parent or carer. They focus on the quality of life that everyone using the service actually experiences.

Using the national care standards

If you are thinking about using early education or childcare services, you will want to refer to the standards to help you decide about them.

Providers will use the standards to find out what is expected of them in offering childcare and early education services. The standards make it clear that everything about the service should lead to you and your child enjoying good quality services. They should guide the provider over who to employ and how they should manage the service.

These national care standards provide the framework for assessing the service as a whole. They cover a wide range of care services from babies to teenagers. The way in which the standards are to be met in a particular case will depend on the type of provision being inspected. The Scottish Commission for the Regulation of Care ('the Care Commission') has discretion to apply the standards flexibly, taking into account the nature of the service.

Where centres are funded for pre-school education, the quality indicators of *The Child at the Centre* and the *Curriculum Framework for Children 3-5* also help to describe national expectations. In particular, these provide advice about the curriculum, children's progress, assessment, support for learning and quality assurance.

The principles behind the standards

The standards reflect the rights of children and young people, as set down in the UN Convention on the Rights of the Child. They also reflect the general principles applying to all the standards developed by the National Care Standards Committee. The principles themselves are not standards but reflect the recognised rights which children, young people, parents and carers enjoy as citizens. These principles are the result of all the contributions made by the National Care Standards Committee, its working groups and everyone else who responded to the consultations on the standards as they were being written. They recognise that services must be accessible and suitable for everyone who needs them, including people from black and ethnic minority communities and children with disabilities. They reflect the strong agreement that children and young people's experience of the services is very important and should be positive.

The main principles are dignity, privacy, choice, safety, realising potential and equality and diversity. Users of the service have a right to:

Dignity
- be treated with dignity and respect at all times; and
- enjoy a full range of social relationships.

Privacy
- have your privacy and property respected; and
- be free from unnecessary intrusion.

Choice
- make informed choices, while recognising the rights of other people to do the same; and
- know about the range of choices.

Safety
- feel safe and secure in all aspects of life, including health and wellbeing;
- enjoy safety but not be over-protected; and
- be free from exploitation and abuse.

Realising potential

- achieve all you can;

- make full use of the resources that are available to you; and

- make the most of your life.

Equality and diversity

- live an independent life, rich in purpose, meaning and personal fulfilment;

- be valued for your ethnic background, language, culture and faith;

- be treated equally and to live in an environment which is free from bullying, harassment and discrimination; and

- be able to complain effectively without fear of victimisation.

The Scottish Commission for the Regulation of Care

The Regulation of Care (Scotland) Act 2001 ('the Act') set up the Care Commission, which registers and inspects all the services regulated under the Act, taking account of the national care standards issued by Scottish Ministers. The Care Commission has its headquarters in Dundee, with regional offices across the country. It will assess applications from people who want to provide early education and childcare services. It will inspect the services to make sure that they are meeting the regulations and in doing so will take account of the national care standards. You can find out more about the Care Commission and what it does from its website (www.carecommission.com).

The Scottish Social Services Council

The Act created the Scottish Social Services Council ('the Council') which was established on 1 October 2001. It also has its headquarters in Dundee. The Council has the duty of promoting high standards of conduct and practice among social services workers, and in their education and training. To deliver its overall aims of protecting service users and carers and securing the confidence of the public in social services, the Council has been given five main tasks. These are: to establish registers of key groups of social services staff; to publish codes of practice for all social services staff and their employers; to regulate the conduct of registered workers; to regulate the training and education of the workforce; to undertake the functions of the National Training Organisation for the Personal Social Services. The Council has issued codes of practice for social service workers and employers of social service workers. These describe the standards of conduct and practice within which they should work. The codes are available from the Council website (www.sssc.uk.com).

How standards and regulations work together

The Act gives Scottish Ministers the power to publish standards which the Care Commission must take into account when making its decisions. It also gives Scottish Ministers the power to make regulations imposing requirements in relation to early education and childcare services.

The standards will be taken into account by the Care Commission in making any decision about applications for registration (including varying or removing a condition that may have been imposed on the registration of the service). All providers must provide a statement of function and purpose when they are applying to register their service. On the basis of that statement, the Care Commission will determine which standards will apply to the service that the provider is offering.

The standards will be used to monitor the quality of services and their compliance with the Act and the regulations. If, at inspection, or at other times, for example, as a result of the Care Commission looking into a complaint, there are concerns about the service, the Care Commission will take the standards into account in any decision on whether to take enforcement action and what action to take.

If the standards were not being fully met, the Care Commission would note this in the inspection report and require the service manager to address this. The Care Commission could impose an additional condition on the service's registration if the provider persistently, substantially or seriously failed to meet the standards or breached a regulation. If the provider does not then meet the condition, the Care Commission could issue an improvement notice detailing the required improvement to be made and the timescale for this. Alternatively, the Care Commission could move straight to an improvement notice. The Care Commission would move to cancel the registration of any service if the improvement notice does not achieve the desired result. In extreme cases (i.e. where there is serious risk to a person's life, health or wellbeing) the Care Commission could take immediate steps to cancel the registration of any service without issuing an improvement notice.

Regulations are mandatory. In some cases not meeting a regulation will be an offence. This means a provider may be subject to prosecution. Not meeting or breaching any regulation is a serious matter.

Decisions by the Care Commission on what to do when standards or regulations are not met will take into account all the relevant circumstances and be proportionate.

You can get information on these regulations from the *Regulation of Care (Scotland) Act 2001*, which is available from the Stationery Office Bookshop at a cost of £7.95 a copy. You can also see the Act on-line (see Annex B for the address).

You can also see the Scottish Statutory Instruments for the Regulation of Care Regulations 2002 on-line (see Annex B for the address).

Terms used

To help you understand the standards, here is an explanation of some of the terms used:

- **staff** includes any person caring for children and young people, including childminders and managers, whether volunteers, self-employed or paid employees;

- **manager** is the person responsible for the daily management of the service;

- **person in charge** is the person who provides the service and has overall responsibility for it; and

- **you** is used to refer to parents, carers and/or children and young people as appropriate. It reflects the rights of children and young people to be at the centre of the care provided but also acknowledges parents' and carers' rights, particularly in respect of young children.

Comments

If you would like to comment on these standards you can visit our website and send a message through our mailbox:

www.scotland.gov.uk/health/standardsandsponsorship

You can also contact us at:

Care Standards and Sponsorship Branch
Community Care Division
Health Department
St Andrew's House
Regent Road
Edinburgh EH1 3AG

Tel: 0131 244 3520
Fax: 0131 244 4005

1-3

Being welcomed and cared for

1 Being welcomed and valued
2 A safe environment
3 Health and wellbeing

national**care**standards
early education and childcare up to the age of 16

Being welcomed and valued

Standard 1

Each child or young person will be welcomed, and will be valued as an individual.

1 You can be confident that staff welcoming children or young people have the time to do so, and are trained to do so, well.

2 Parents and carers and children or young people as appropriate are provided with information about the service in a language and format that they can understand.

3 Parents and carers and children or young people have opportunities to visit the service before using it.

A safe environment

Standard 2

The needs of each child or young person are met by the service in a safe environment, in line with all relevant legislation.

1 Children and young people are cared for in a safe, hygienic, smoke-free, pleasant and stimulating environment. The surroundings are in a good state of decoration and repair.

2 Children and young people have access to accommodation which is secure and suitable to meet the needs of all users. Arrangements are in place to make sure of the safety and security of children and young people, inside and outside.

3 Children and young people enjoy the service in an environment that takes account of the space standards in Annex A and makes effective use of space, including outdoor play areas. The layout allows for areas where they can play and work independently, meet with a small number of others or be part of a larger group.

4 You can be confident that:

- the service conforms to all other relevant legislation on accommodation and facilities;

- staff keep all play equipment clean and well maintained;

- staff take measures to control the spread of infection; and

- staff make sure that children and young people do not have access to inappropriate materials, including screening access to the internet.

Health and wellbeing

Standard 3

Each child or young person will be nurtured by staff who will promote his or her general wellbeing, health, nutrition and safety.

1 Children and young people can be assured of continuity of care in the service through effective communication between the staff, children and young people and parents and carers, and any other relevant service providers.

2 You can be confident that staff have a clear understanding of their roles and responsibilities in protecting children and young people from harm, abuse, bullying and neglect. The service has a policy on child protection and safety and explains the policies to parents and carers and each child or young person.

3 Children and young people have opportunities to learn about healthy lifestyles and relationships, hygiene, diet and personal safety.

4 Children and young people have access to a well-balanced and healthy diet (where food is provided) which takes account of ethnic, cultural and dietary requirements, including food allergies. Staff make sure that help with feeding is given in a way that best meets the needs of the child or young person.

5 Children and young people have the opportunity to sleep or rest and have regular access to fresh air and energetic physical play. Staff will monitor sleeping children regularly and effectively.

6 You can be confident that the service has a clear policy and guidelines on the use, storage and administration of medication and that staff are suitably trained to carry these out. The service makes sure that written consent is given by parents and carers for the use or administration of medication provided by them.

7 You can be confident that the service has a clear policy on how to deal with emergencies and staff are well trained in emergency procedures.

4-11

Confidence in the service

national**care**standards
early education and childcare up to the age of 16

Engaging with children

Standard 4

Each child or young person will be supported by staff who interact effectively and enthusiastically with him or her.

1 You can expect staff to have a good understanding of the stages of children and young people's development and learning.

2 Children and young people receive support and care from staff who understand the significance of high quality interaction. This develops the quality of all activities, including play and leisure.

3 You can be confident that staff will interact with children and young people in a way that builds confidence, extends learning and encourages and values their contributions.

4 You can be confident that the staff will:

- regularly assess the development and learning of each child and young person;

- use this assessment information to plan the next steps in the child or young person's development and learning; and

- share this information with the child or young person as appropriate, with parents and carers and others professionally involved in the child or young person's development.

Quality of experience

Standard 5

Each child or young person can experience and choose from a balanced range of activities.

1 Children and young people can experience and choose from programmes and day-to-day activities that are planned, designed, evaluated and put into practice by staff, taking account of national and local guidelines.

2 Children and young people will be able to enjoy the activities and be motivated by them. The activities will be flexible and take account of ages, development needs, interests, and hours and patterns of attendance of each child or young person.

3 You know that the activities provided by staff will allow the children and young people to enjoy both organised and free play and leisure and recreation, including quiet times.

4 Children and young people will have opportunities to express their views, exercise choice and, where possible, influence the programme.

5 Children and young people will be able to interact with others or play or work individually.

6 The progress in children and young people's development will be regularly monitored by staff, who will use this information to improve the programme.

Support and development

Standard 6

Each child or young person receives support from staff who respond to his or her individual needs.

1   You can be confident that staff are flexible and responsive to children and young people's personal, emotional, educational and physical needs. They are responsive to the support needs of children, young people and families and are sensitive to individual circumstances including disabilities.

2   You know that staff will work effectively with parents, carers and children and young people to support each individual child or young person's development and learning.

3   You know that staff will establish effective working relationships with support agencies. These may include medical services, teachers, therapists, educational psychologists and learning support staff and social workers.

4   You know that staff will draw up and put into practice individualised educational programmes and plans to support children, young people and families where appropriate. They will do this in consultation with parents and carers, children and young people and professionals.

5   You can be confident that staff are knowledgeable about, and have a clear understanding of, relevant legislation relating to children and young people, including those with special needs.

6   You have help to use services, aids and equipment for communication if your first language is not English or if you have any other communication needs.

A caring environment

Standard 7

In using the service, children, young people, parents and carers experience an environment of mutual respect, trust and open communication.

1 Parents, carers, children and young people receive information about the aims and values of the service in a language and format you can easily understand. Staff actively promote these aims and values. The service has a clear code of behaviour, which is consistently applied by staff and understood by staff, parents and carers, children and young people. Children and young people are encouraged to take responsibility for their own behaviour and to show care and consideration for others.

2 You experience a service where mutual trust, respect, confidence and a caring ethos are evident.

3 Children and young people are consulted about the service provided and their views and ideas are valued. They are generally happy and confident.

4 You can be confident that staff will establish positive working relationships with each other and with parents and carers, children and young people.

5 You can be confident that staff will work in partnership with parents and carers to promote positive behaviour and deal with difficult behaviour. Staff will challenge and respond to bullying and discrimination. This will be done in a caring and sensitive manner without threatening or using physical punishment or emotional or verbal abuse.

6 Parents and carers will be encouraged to take part in the service, with staff establishing an effective partnership and keeping in regular communication. Staff will value and take account of parents' and carers' knowledge and views of their child's development needs, interests and personality.

7 If you make an enquiry or a complaint, staff will deal with it efficiently and effectively and provide full information about what will happen as a result of the complaint. You will not be penalised in any way by the service if you have made a complaint. You can talk to staff in private.

Equality and fairness

Standard 8

You will be treated equally and fairly.

1 You can be confident that staff will make sure that all children and young people, parents, carers and the members of staff themselves are treated with respect and in a fair and just way, respecting the needs and characteristics of the individual.

2 You know that staff will assist families who experience difficulties in accessing support services.

3 If parents and carers face any barriers which prevent them from playing an effective part in their child's care and education, staff will work to reduce these barriers.

Involving the community

Standard 9

You can be confident that the service contributes to the community and looks for opportunities to be involved in the community.

1 You know that the service:

- contributes to the life of the community;

- has effective links with community organisations;

- makes information about its provision readily available to members of the community;

- makes efforts to provide information to you about community resources;

- knows about and makes effective use of community facilities (where appropriate); and

- provides opportunities for children and young people to take part in the wider community.

Involving other services

Standard 10

You can be confident that the service keeps up links and works effectively with partner organisations.

1 You benefit from:

- the well-developed links between the service and other relevant childcare services, schools and agencies such as health and social work services in the local area; and

- the way in which the service links with relevant national and local organisations.

Access to resources

Standard 11

Each child or young person has access to a sufficient and suitable range of resources.

1 Children and young people have access to equipment and materials – including multi-cultural materials – which are effectively organised by staff and used to support key aspects of children and young people's development and learning.

2 Children and young people's interests are encouraged through displays that are attractively presented and include a variety of examples made by them. Staff change the material regularly.

3 Children and young people find their quality of experience enhanced by the effective use made of skills and ideas from staff, parents and carers, the children and young people themselves, and from visitors.

4 Children and young people benefit from the use that staff make of a range of outside resources and information and communication technology.

12-14

Confidence in management

nationalcarestandards
early education and childcare up to the age of 16

Confidence in staff

Standard 12

Each child or young person receives support and care from staff who are competent and confident and who have gone through a careful selection procedure.

1 You can be confident that the service recruits and selects staff and volunteers through a process which takes account of safe recruitment practices. These include:

- enhanced disclosures from Disclosure Scotland;

- checks with previous employer;

- taking up references; and

- cross-referencing to the register of the Scottish Social Services Council or other professional organisations.

2 You can be confident that the service:

- complies with the input standards on adult:child ratios and staff qualifications in Annex A;

- applies procedures to select staff with a range of qualifications, skills and experience relevant to the aims of the service;

- provides staffing levels which are sufficient to provide for the needs of children and young people and allow for continuity of care;

- uses staff in ways that make good use of their expertise; and

- has an effective system for identifying and monitoring staff development needs; training is carefully planned and evaluated in line with national and local guidelines.

Improving the service

Standard 13

You can be confident that the service will evaluate what it does and make improvements.

1 You can be confident that:

- staff are involved in the systematic evaluation and discussion of their work and the work of the service, including the use of assessment information;

- parents/carers, children, young people and staff will have the opportunity to contribute as appropriate to evaluation;

- evaluation is continuous and takes account of relevant national and local advice; and

- staff will have clear plans for maintaining and improving the service.

Well-managed service

Standard 14

You can be confident that you are using a service that is well managed.

1 You know that the manager makes sure that management responsibility and accountability are well defined and communicated.

2 You can be confident that the records, plans and policies are properly made and kept in accordance with national and local guidance. These should include:

- details of the aims and objectives of the service;

- admission criteria and process;

- charges;

- complaints procedure;

- accident and incident reports;

- injury insurance;

- contact details;

- confidentiality;

- emergency procedures;

- child protection policy; and

- whistle-blowing.

3 You know who the person in charge is and how to contact them.

4 You can be confident that the manager demonstrates effective leadership qualities and communication skills and fosters effective working relationships between staff, with parents and carers and with children and young people.

5 Parents and carers, children and young people are encouraged to make a full contribution to the life and work of the service.

6 You can be confident that the manager demonstrates a high level of professional competence and skill and a thorough understanding of childcare issues.

7 You know that the person in charge and senior staff monitor effectively the quality of work of each member of staff and the service as a whole.

Annex A

national**care**standards
early education and childcare up to the age of 16

Annex A

Input standards

1 Adult:Child ratios in non-domestic premises

The ratios apply to new providers from 1 April 2002. Existing providers are expected to achieve the new ratios by 1 April 2004.

Age	Ratio
Under 2s	1:3
2 to under 3s	1:5
*3 and over	1:8
If all children are 8 or over	1:10

* Where children aged 3 and over attend facilities providing day care for a session which is less than a continuous period of four hours in any day the adult: child ratio may be 1:10. providing individual children do not attend more than one session per day.

Two adults to be in attendance at any one time.

Only adults in contact with children for the majority of the session should count towards the ratios.

The regulator would be able to vary the ratios up or down where warranted for example attendance of children with special needs, awkward premises and additional support staff on the premises.

2 Adult:Child ratios in domestic premises

1:6 for children under 12, of whom no more than three are not yet attending primary school and of whom no more than one is under 1.

These ratios include the childminder's own children. The Care Commission will have regard to the number of children aged 12 to 16 who are likely to be in the house regularly, and will have the discretion to vary the ratios accordingly. The Care Commission will also have discretion to vary the ratios to take account of special circumstances, such as siblings under 1, special needs, awkward premises, etc.

3 Qualified staff

The intention is to move to a position where all staff in centres providing childcare or pre-school education either hold an appropriate qualification, are seeking accreditation of skills and experience or are pursuing on-the-job training with a view to registering with the Scottish Social Services Council in due course. The Council published its qualification requirements for registration of the early years workforce in March 2004, and will begin phased registration of the workforce during 2006. Employers are advised to develop training plans in order to meet the expectations set out in Standard 12 and help their staff meet registration requirements. For further information see Annex C.

4 Space standards in non-domestic premises

The School Premises (General Requirement and Standards) (Scotland) Regulations 1967 (as amended) continue to apply to nursery schools under the management of education authorities.

For all other non-domestic childcare, the following space standards apply, although the Care Commission will have discretion to vary the standards to take account of special circumstances.

Age	Space
Under 2s	3.7 square metres
2 to under 3s	2.8 square metres
3 and over	2.3 square metres

Annex B

national**care**standards
early education and childcare up to the age of 16

Annex B

Useful reference material

Legal

The Children (Scotland) Act 1995

The Act puts children first. Each child has the right to:

- be treated as an individual;
- form and express views on matters affecting him or her; and
- be protected from all forms of abuse, neglect or exploitation.

Parents and local authorities have rights and responsibilities in achieving the balance of care.

The Act is accompanied by four volumes of regulations and guidance, *Scotland's Children (1997)*.

The Data Protection Act 1998

The Act covers how information about living, identifiable people is used. All organisations that hold or process personal data must comply.

The Disability Discrimination Act 1995

This wide-ranging Act, which came into force in 1996, makes it illegal to discriminate against disabled people in employment, access to goods, services, transport and education.

Fire Precautions (Workplace) Regulations 1997 (as amended)

The Regulations place a responsibility on employers for carrying out risk assessments in relation to premises. The risk assessment is a means of providing fire precautions for the safety of people using the premises.

The Health and Safety at Work etc Act 1974

The Act is the basic piece of health and safety law that covers everyone who is affected by work activity. It places the burden of legal responsibility for health and safety at work with the employer.

The Human Rights Act 1998

The Act incorporates the European Convention on Human Rights into Scots and English law in relation to the acts of public bodies. Its purpose is to protect human rights and to maintain and promote the ideals and values of a democratic society. The Articles of Convention include:

- freedom of thought, conscience and religion;
- freedom of expression;
- freedom of assembly and association;
- the right to have respect for private and family life; and
- the right to marry.

The Misuse of Drugs Act 1971

The Act is the main law for drugs control in the UK. It prohibits the possession, supply and manufacture of medicinal and other products except where these have been made legal by the Misuse of Drugs Regulations 1985. The legislation is concerned with controlled drugs and puts these into five separate schedules. Anyone who is responsible for storing or administering controlled drugs should be aware of the content of the Misuse of Drugs Regulations 1985 and the Misuse of Drugs (Safe Custody) Regulations 1973.

The Police Act 1997

Part V of the Police Act 1997 was implemented in April 2002. This provides for Disclosure Scotland at the Scottish Criminal Record Office to issue disclosure certificates to individuals and organisations. For those regularly caring for, training, or being in sole charge of children, the certificates will include details of all convictions and any other information which the police consider relevant to the post. When the Index of Adults Unsuitable to work with children is established, any information from this list will be included too.

The Public Interest Disclosure Act 1998

The Act protects workers who 'blow the whistle' about wrongdoing. It mainly takes the form of amendments to the Employment Rights Act 1996, and makes provision about the kinds of disclosures which may be protected; the circumstances in which such disclosures are protected; and the persons who may be protected.

The Race Relations Act 1976

The Act makes racial discrimination illegal in employment, service delivery, training and other areas.

The Race Relations (Amendment) Act 2000

The Act makes racial discrimination illegal in public activities that were not previously covered. It puts a general duty on public organisations to promote race equality.

The Regulation of Care (Scotland) Act 2001

The Act establishes a new system of care service regulation including the registration and inspection of care services which takes account of national care standards. The Act also creates two new national, independent bodies, the Scottish Commission for the Regulation of Care, to regulate care services, and the Scottish Social Services Council, to regulate the social service workforce and to promote and regulate its education and training.

You can visit these websites for information:

- Regulation of Care (Scotland) Act 2001
www.scotland-legislation.hmso.gov.uk/legislation/scotland/acts2001/20010008.htm

- Regulation of Care (Scotland) Act 2001 Statutory Instruments
www.scotland-legislation.hmso.gov.uk/legislation/scotland/s-200201.htm

The Rehabilitation of Offenders Act 1974

The Act enables some criminal convictions to become 'spent' or ignored, after a rehabilitation period. The rehabilitation period is a set length of time from the date of conviction.

The Sex Discrimination Act 1975

The Sex Discrimination Act 1975 makes it unlawful to discriminate on grounds of sex or marital status in recruitment, promotion and training. The Act also covers education, the provision of housing, goods and services and advertising.

Standards in Scotland's Schools etc, Act 2000

Local authorities are required to have regard to the guidance issued under Section 34 when exercising their duties in relation to pre-school education. The guidance recognises the importance of delivering quality services for children and expects pre-school education not only to make a distinctive contribution but to link into the wider efforts to secure integrated services for children and families.

Policy

Aiming for Excellence: Modernising Social Work Services in Scotland 1999

The White Paper sets out the proposals to strengthen the protection of children and vulnerable adults and to make sure high quality services are provided. The Scottish Commission for the Regulation of Care is an independent regulator set up for this purpose.

Our National Health 2000

The health plan aims to improve Scotland's health and close the health gap between rich and poor, restoring the NHS as a national service and improving care and standards.

Other useful references

The UN Convention on the Rights of the Child

The Convention is not a law but a code that the Government signed up to in 1991. It recognises that young people under 18 in Scotland do have rights. These rights must be given fairly, and children and young people must be kept safe and well, and able to take part in society.

A Curriculum Framework for Children 3-5
The Scottish Consultative Council on the Curriculum, 1999.

The Child at the Centre
Scottish Executive Education Department, 2000. A good practice guide for all providers of care and education for 3 to 5 year olds.

A Manual of Good Practice in Special Educational Needs
Scottish Office Education and Industry Department, 1998. A manual of guidance to all those concerned with the education of children and young people with special educational needs. It includes advice for pre-school teachers.

Guidance on Teacher Involvement in Pre-School Education
Issued by the Scottish Executive Education Department in January 2002, will in due course be subsumed within the statutory guidance offered to local authorities under section 34 of the Standards in Scotland's Schools etc, Act 2000.

Annex C

national**care**standards
early education and childcare up to the age of 16

Annex C

Information on SSSC registration

In March 2004 the Scottish Social Services Council (SSSC) set the qualification requirements for early education and childcare workers for registration with the SSSC.

Since there are a wide range of job titles used in the sector the SSSC has categorised the parts of the Register for early education and childcare workers on the basis of job functions. Therefore, there will be a part of the Register for each of the following categories of early education and childcare workers:

Support workers are workers who have delegated responsibility for providing care and support to children.

Practitioners are workers who identify and meet the care, support and learning needs of children and contribute to the development and quality assurance of informal learning activities and/or curriculum. They may also be responsible for the supervision of other workers.

Managers/lead practitioners are workers who hold responsibilities for the overall development, management and quality assurance of service provision including the supervision of staff and the management of resources.

Examples of jobs in early childcare and childcare linked to categories for registration

Support Worker	Practitioner	Lead Practitioner/Manager
seasonal play worker	play leader	manager
nursery assistant	nursery nurse	officer in charge
play assistant	nursery officer	co-ordinator
support for learning assistant	nursery assistant	play manager
breakfast club assistant	play assistant	early years manager
wraparound care assistant	playgroup worker	out-of-school care co-ordinator
	early education and childcare worker	
	early years worker	

Applicants for registration who do not hold a required qualification may, if they meet all the other eligibility criteria for registration, be granted registration subject to the condition that they achieve the required qualification within a specified period of time, normally the first three years of the registration period. Access to registration will have to be gradual to allow sufficient time for workers to access and achieve the required qualifications.

There is a range of qualifications that can meet the requirement for registration. To obtain a copy of the full list go to www.sssc.uk.com or telephone 01382 207101 or email enquiries@sssc.uk.com